Cast Iron Butterflies

finding peace, hope, and joy, day by day

Mykal Ward

To Patty, wishing, hoping, and praying for your continued blessings, and peace beyond any understanding.
— M

 # dedications . . .

to those of you who feel alone or invisible…
who feel trapped and helpless,
and haven't seen peace or joy in so long
you've forgotten how they feel…

please be encouraged.
there is another side, and you will get there.

to the me I used to be, the me who I'm becoming,
and all those who have walked with me along this journey;
I love and appreciate you beyond measure.

these words

These words,
in this book,
aren't for everyone…
In fact,
that fact
almost kept
this book
from happening.

But
every time
I tried
to hide them away,
these words
cried out
as if needing escape…
or release.

These words said,
"don't forget
your promise…
and don't forget
who this is about."
"Remember…"

And I do.
I remember
being there, all alone,
wondering how I got there
and how on earth I would ever get out.
I remember searching and searching

for safety, for peace, a hand to hold…
Someone to say,

Yes, I too have been there,
where you are,
and I made it out…
So can you.

in these pages...

Me Time ... 7
thought processes, healing, revelations, vulnerabilities, awareness, & the beginning stages of freedom

5 - 7 - 5 ... 58
45 haiku poems, mostly focused on thought life, reflections, & realizations

Relationship Status ... 73
about an attempt to move forward in love and relationships

Lifted ... 107
intended to encourage, lift, celebrate, & empower...

– me time –

pause

I earnestly embrace
every thought
and emotion.

I pause and allow each to be.

It's just, some I allow to linger.
and others I choose to set free.

note to self:

It really is ok to be
all of who you are
right now

on the way
to who
you are becoming

no way.

If I went back in time
and told the old me
where she'd be today
there's no way she would
believe me.

She'd probably just
smile wistfully
and say,

"No way..."

without conditions

The more I
acknowledge,
accept and
embrace who I am...
the closer I get
to healing.

See –
I have to love it all,
the way a mother
loves her child –
   without conditions;
   no ifs ands or buts

and you can't love it all,
without accepting it all...
So yeah.

I love all of me.
and that is
how I will heal.

I will love
the introvert
and the empath,
the peacemaker
and the teacher,
the horrified misfit
the confused little black girl
the brokenhearted

the single mom,
and the one who's
sometimes afraid of crowds;
the trapped and the guarded,
the curious and the weary,
the sufferer, the survivor,
and the misunderstood.

I will love all of me
every bit... every day.
and that will take me
all the way home...

not really ok

Maybe I should've
called out for help.
Sometimes I
wonder why I didn't.
It didn't seem
   to be an option,
      I suppose…

So I
disappeared,
and they let me.
No one came to visit.
No one called.

and so it was.

Before the abuse,
I was already me:
Introvert. Quiet. Reserved.
sort of in my own world.

and now… after it all,
the world feels so cold,
and full of blank faces,
or what's worse – facades –
expressions hiding truth
  in a way
   that keeps me
    bundled up.

So, sometimes, I really
just don't want to go.
I'm tired. and I'm... recovering.
and these people don't even get it.

I don't want to be around them,
because it's exhausting.
and it's painful.

Everything hurts...
Even when I'm feeling ok.
Even though I'm on the mend.

Because I'm not....

...I'm not really ok.

Maybe that's it.
I'm not as
ok as I
have to
seem to be.

and maybe
pretending
is part of the pain.

motherhood, now

She follows my lead.
I should
probably
try harder
  to walk
    in one
      direction.

I forget that I knew...

The highs and lows
never cease
to amaze me.

Somewhere
in my thoughts,
I know both exist...

highs & lows...
ups & downs...

I'm even aware
of the twists & turns.

But when each shows up,
it's a marvel to me still.

Somehow
I forget ...
that I knew
it was coming.

quiet

Sometimes,
I have
so much to say,
but something
keeps me silent...

At times,
I just want
to cry, or scream,
but it gets lost
on the way out…

I smile, I chat, I
make small talk,
and sometimes…

I try to be so quiet
that no one notices me.

Yet, inside, I'm screaming:
"This isn't fair!"
"Why is life so hard?"
"Help me, please!"

But since I'm so old
and that stuff
sounds like a kid,
Maybe that's
why I stay

Quiet.

trying

I spend too much time and energy

~wishing for more~
trying to convince myself
I shouldn't,

because I am enough…

… and trying to believe it.

pulse monitor

Sometimes,
I forget what it feels like to laugh…

I spend so much time
combating stress
and anxiety…
so much time
~ just getting by.
chasing
serenity & sanity,
as though
they were both
fleeing notions.

and when, on occasion,
I hear myself laugh…

I mean that
real, authentic,
deep down in my heart laugh…
that laugh that
energizes, radiates,
and escapes without warning…

When I hear myself laugh like that,
    it's like a pulse monitor…
    or that machine in the hospital…
    letting me know – I'm alive.

opposing corners

feels sort of like
apathy and anxiety
are eyeing each other

from opposing corners
of my mind…

I wonder
who'll serve
as referee…

through the deafening silence

We wonder why no one
comes running to help…

I think we forget –
we've muffled our screams...
donned superhuman capes...
& manufactured these
genuine smiles....

I mean,
it's not like we'd know
how to ask
for the help that we need…

& through the
deafening silence,
we can still hear.

almost

and I'm standing
right here
at the edge of this
feeling

at the onset
of this emotion

intrigued...
almost ready;
knowing what needs
to be done

Yet, I stand still.
I don't dare venture on.

Who knows where
this path will take me?
Who knows
if I'll ever return?

not easy to be

It's so extremely
exhausting.
   pretending
   performing
   mustering up this
   semblance
   of health;

all the while
knowing
and feeling...
way down deep
in my bones:

I'm not really ok.

I mean, I am.
Really... Sincerely I am.

But my goodness,
It's not easy to be.

Making "ok" look so
natural…

It steals my breath,

just attempting to
explain.

unspoken

Sometimes I wonder
If me, being me,
has created
her Silence…

Sometimes, I wonder
if she has more
to say.

thought struggle

There's always
this struggle
   between
      the thought
I'm thinking

& the one
I should be

lost thoughts

I keep chasing
lost thoughts
& I don't
know why.

If they are
meant for me,
they won't
stay away.

now

right now
I'm ...
learning how
to let now
just be now…

…just for now.

scattered pieces

Maybe all these
scattered pieces

really do
add up

to the whole

Me.

untitled

to those of you
who've lived abuse –

if you've ever
thought back
& asked,

"Was it really
so bad, after all?"

I can tell you:

it was.

complexity

I'm not really
all that complex;
what you see
is what you get

It's just...
quite simply –

most folks
can't see me.

turning pages

fighting between
turning pages
and flat out
skipping chapters

I want to see
what's next
see where all of this
will take me

I want to be
past this already.

No, listen....
I'm saying WAY past this –
& not just by a page....

I want to be living
in the sequel
already.

note to self

You have to want it gone.
You can't wrap up
in this feeling
& then wonder why
it stays.

untitled

All of
the things
I thought
would
end me...

didn't.

& neither
will this.

let them go

If they leave,
let them.

they must not belong
in your story.

and if they used to belong,
maybe their part is just over.

If they leave,
let them go.

and you just
keep being
you.

speechless

She said,

"Hmmmmmm....
So you think
it's a character flaw
to have various aspects
to who you are...

It's as if you feel
there's only one
right way for you
to be."

I paused...

turned her
thoughts around
a time or two,
but couldn't answer.

I was angry at myself,
because that's
what I did believe.

& I was angry
at whoever
taught me to believe it.

She said,
"I think it's wonderful.
You're so multifaceted...
so dynamic."

I wanted to respond,
but never found the words.

current coordinates

This is not the life
that I imagined...
Truth be told,
I don't know
what life I did.

I just know this isn't it.

but here I am,
and somehow I know...
behind the pain;
behind the questions

the healing source
& all the answers
wait in patience –

as I unfold the truth:

this is right where
I'm supposed
to be.

lost and found

Be careful what you look for.

You will find it.

& sometimes,
you don't truly know
what you've been looking for

until years after you found it...

until you wake up
and realize

you found
what you were looking for
...many years ago

& that's the problem.
You found it...

you just didn't realize
you'd been seeking
so much pain...

Life is funny like that.

You should've
been looking
for something else
all along.

when will I learn?

I do too much for others
and for their applause

& they never asked me to.

When will I learn
to stand up and cheer
for myself?

yet

She's smart.
& she watches me.
I feel her wondering
if I'm ok.

I want to tell her, yes
but I'm not sure
if that's true...
yet.

impatience

Give it time.
you'll understand
who I am
if you stick around
long enough.

I never did
quite
get along
with impatience.

a question

I'm getting
tired of
getting to the
bottom
of things.

Why can't they
come up here
and find me?

crowded

I can't decide
which crowds
my mind most...
is it the ebbs
or the flows?

surrender

She let go
& collapsed.
said, "That's it,
I'm done...
I give up."

& just then,
in that moment,
the true work
began.

staged

I think I smile
so much
because
I'm afraid
you'll try
to help me
if I just
walk around
wearing
my true self

& that's why
life is so
exhausting.
my whole day is
spent
on stage.

student life

He tells me
he's like this
because he's lived
a life of trauma.
She says
she wants to learn
to be herself.
He has so much
to say – but
can't seem to get
  the words to fit
into a safe place.
She reluctantly, crying,
hands me a letter
to someone (from her)
Says.... I don't know
who to give this to.
Suicidal Thoughts
& Failure...
decorate the page.
He disappears to Texas
without a real goodbye.
She asks
to leave the room
every time I tell her:
"Hey, you're missing work."
He can't focus,

She's just mean,
and I don't know
why.

& now it's time to learn
all about ancient Egypt...
Pharaohs and sun gods;
& then it's pronouns...
subject or object –
and we're all just
sitting here...
like this is ok.

enough

& I wish
It didn't take
so long

for enough
to become
ENOUGH.

everybody's okay

I just want to get away
or maybe
I want to scream
or cry…

but I look around, and I see:
everybody's okay --
so I must be okay, too.

slow magic

I'm so
mesmerized
by this
slow magic . . . . .
watching myself
as I
disappear.

Come, watch in
amazement –
come see...
come and see.
The fading
so slight
but right
before your eyes.

No.   Stay.
Give it time.
Can't you see?

* * * * *

They
never stay
long enough
to believe.

how high?

Can't wrap my thoughts
around why...

You haven't even said, "jump"
& I'm already asking
"How high?"

which me?

& I hate the way
I think of you
   first
   all the time

...like I can't
just be me

without
asking myself
   which me
   you'd like
   to see.

judgment free

never been one
to judge,
or the type
to criticize.
    I overstand.
    I go beyond
understanding.

With all that I've
been through
& the mark
it's carved,
I don't think
I'll ever blink
at anyone's
demeanor.

We become,
who we become.

these walls

How can I be so
comfortable
   & safe
within these walls,
but also
yearning
to escape them?

faith and patience

Faith and Patience
leaned in
toward me
& whispered

(in unison)

> "Precious Heart,
> you must find
> your own dreams
> to tend to."

untitled

I think,
sometimes –
I get tired
of bracing
    for impact.

Sometimes,
it's like, eff it.

    Let it come.

impossibly free

I look back sometimes
Just to check in
with the facts
the same ones
I denied, then owned.
Yes, it was that bad
Yes I nearly lost myself

Yes, I did get away.
Yes, I did survive.

I never ever ever
would have believed
I'd be this free.

when she says hello

She lies dormant all day
and then gently awakes,
just as the world
starts its bedtime routine.

This is when she says – hello
... when she sees, hears and speaks

Now, she can't sleep.
She's got so much to say.

I call her: Voice

5 - 7 - 5

1.

Wisdom wears no mask
often hiding in plain sight
too bright to be seen

2.

Suddenly I am
juxtaposing two and two;
the aha moment

3.

What if I told you ~
these can be the hardest days
and the best days, too?

4.

Wisdom keeps playing
Marco Polo in the pool
– never learned to swim

5.

Distracting myself
from the lies my thoughts tell me
– whole new way of life

6.

I spend lots of time
arguing with my own thoughts
& sometimes, I win.

7.

What is this feeling?
Incomplete but familiar...
frequent visitor

8.

Yes, I am changing;
but not into something new –
returned to design

9.

Time stood still, waiting –
unconcerned, all of these years –
knowing I'd return.

10.
caught a glimpse of me
it had been such a long time
since I'd seen myself

11.
Sometimes I forget
who I am deep down inside
armor's *safe* disguise

12.
I can hear your voice
It trespasses through the walls
angry at the world

13.

Even as a kid
remedy for loneliness
found in a good book

14.

many beginnings
happen without announcement
one drop in life's pond

15.

Authenticity
should be easier to do
me, just being me

16.
idk I might
be adequately unwell
truth is, I can't tell

17.
here's the thing with lines
knowing where to draw each one
learning not to cross

18.
seems they never stay;
always find someplace to go.
(restless hopes & dreams)

19.

Can't find the middle
all or nothing, either or;
There's no in between.

20.

yeah, we all need one
we all need a wanted thing
something to hope for

21.

I'm like, whatever.
Life gets so arbitrary ...
... might as well just chill

22.

I can't find the words
so I wait quietly here,
where they can find me.

23.

surprise love affair
between structure & freedom
– passionate haiku

24.

All those years ago
we stumbled haphazardly
into each other

25.

& they ask us why
we don't want to fall in love
wounded from the fall

26.

gradually, yes...
enough does become enough
& it's time to go

27.

Never said goodbye;
just sort of faded away...
Our shadows still speak.

28.
won't reach out to you
I'm aware you can't be found
- just a text away

29.
had to let you go
I'm talkin' - all the way 'go'
This is not our time.

30.
I had to let go,
setting free our stubborn hearts
only way to live

31.

Quit playing these games
shred and burn the instructions
I know them by heart.

32.

ev'ry choice I've made,
since the day we walked away,
always wears your name.

33.

I was mistaken –
sometimes goodbye is hello.
Go ahead and go.

34.

You can't have one bit.
I'm the sole proprietor;
go find your own peace.

35.

where will he meet me
if I never step outside
this icy fortress?

36.

the weight of my past
shuffles up and takes a seat
too close for comfort

37.
give your life more time
to become what you hope for
– listen for response

38.
I'm starting to see
forgotten questions find peace
without worry's help.

39.
My heart refuses
to tiptoe safely through life.
– ev'ry step speaks out.

40.
I wake up for you
even when I don't want to
– a peculiar truth

41.
I won't call on you
to fill my empty places;
– they belong to me.

42.
I will let you be
the lesson you came to teach,
no less and no more

43.

busy saving face
we lose sight of our true selves
– nowhere to be found

44.

Let's live the slash life...
We will do/be/live it all
& become the dream

45.

We all start somewhere
just a glimmer in God's eye
& He never blinks

– relationship status –

starting right here

maybe love is possible
even for me, you know?

even for me…

I will love again.
I will be loved.

starting
right here

with me.

my sunshine

you like
how I make you feel...
& I like
how you make me feel;
and that's why
    we won't
      work out.

I can't trust you with
my sunshine.

I have to first be sure
I have enough for me.

guilt-free construction

Truth be told,
I'm actually afraid of you.

I know, it might be silly...
It might be.

Maybe you're harmless.
Maybe you're good for me.
Maybe we're good for each other.
But maybe I'll never know…

See, I've come a long way
and as I've traveled,
I've come to accept...
realize... and understand...
(*not necessarily in that order*)
this notion of self-preservation
this "I'm worth protecting"...
this guilt-free construction pass…

I've granted myself permission
to build as many walls
and board shut as many windows;
seal tight as many cracks
as humanly possible.
And the ones I can't get to yet...
I give those to God.

I've heard it before

and I've read it before....
That classic line:

"I've been *hurt* before."

Yeah... That's pretty awful,
but how about *destroyed?*

There's a whole different feel to:
"*I've been **destroyed** before.*"
Right?

So yeah... I do apologize
if my fears seem unwarranted
and if it feels unfair how I
hold you up to my past,
checking for similarities....

It's just that I
absolutely
refuse
to go back there.

I have no more room
for destruction.
I'm not even done
rebuilding...

But I'll get there.

So for now...
when I see how much
you cared for me,

how much of a great friend
you have been....
I have to hold that
up to the light..........

And that's when I see
the shadows:
You don't even like
yourself.
How can you
love me?

I miss you....
Sometimes I wish
that I didn't...
But I do.

No matter...
Because now
I know better,
and I won't hold onto
anyone
or anything
that threatens my
wholeness /
or my peace.

safety first

I'm not even mad at you.

Yeah, you tried to destroy me.
& you kind of succeeded.
So what?

I'm so ready to rebuild...
So ready for my new life…

I don't have energy
(or time) to waste
being mad at you.

Really... in real life...
I just want you to go away.

you know?

here I am

These are the times I dreaded...
years ago, in captivity.
in his prison...

I told myself:
you'll never get away.
& if you do, how will you survive?

Well, here I am:
surviving.

marionette

Everyone believed the lie
you taught me how to be.
I wasn't real
but no one knew.

I was who you
needed me to be.

My surprise ended early
and they were sad...
... worried even.
but no one came
to say.

They sent cards
and condolences,
but none dared
cross the threshold
of our happy home.

I don't think they were
afraid of you...
I don't know
what they were – – –

just not around.
that's all I knew of them.

They
kept

their distance

to spare themselves...
to spare me...
  – I don't know.

And then you told me:
Look: no one's coming.
It's just you and me.

It broke me
to believe –
I struggled
to believe –
I just needed
to believe –
Something.

So I chose you,
my puppeteer.

I chose to become
fluent in
Deception.

I'm ok
we're ok
it's all so
damned ok.

Sometimes I still
get angry at them
for believing.

forgiveness

I forgave him
because I know
he didn't mean to hurt me
(and oh, did he ever).

He was who he was.
I knew who he was,
& I clung to him still...

Yeah... I know, they're tricky –
masterminds, manipulators....
but they weren't born that way.
I can't fault him
for how he turned out.

Am I pissed that he chose me?
Oh yeah. I'm mad as hell...
but not at him; at me...
for being chosen.

So, I've had to forgive myself
again and again.

I've looked at myself
oh so very close...
because
I need
to know
what he saw in me...

So I can hide it,
until I can change it…

When I say never again....
When I say I refuse to be
hurt that way again....
I've never been
so determined
to honor
a promise.

playbook

I'm so much
stronger now…

and I can see
so much more clearly.

It's like someone
slipped me
the other team's
playbook.

I see
every move
before it's
even played.

mistaken

ah, I see.

you thought my
transparency,
authenticity,
& vulnerability
were synonymous
with weakness.

you saw
an easy target.

no... you were mistaken.

I've upgraded...
leveled up...
I've learned
  to see you
    as you are

and me - as I truly am.
stronger, wiser,
& resilient;
not so easily broken.

How could you
break me?
You'll never
  get close enough
  to even feel me.

inside job

Stop trying to
rescue me.
I've decided
that's
an inside job.

Ignore my
smoke signal
& my S.O.S.

I was
sending those
to myself.

almost

I think one of my
favorite side effects
of abuse
is this new
refusal to trust.
I watch you
(all of you) now –
waiting...
taking note;
asking myself
all the questions
I'd ask you,
if you weren't
so suspect....
Giving you less
than an inch,
because I'll be damned
if you make it a mile
... It's almost like a game
almost funny
... almost fun.

almost.

lucky you

You were never
over it...
Just looking for
someplace
to put it.

Lucky you.
You found me.

limited vision

I fell in love
with the sound
of his laughter.
His joy,
in spite of it all.

In fact,
I marveled so
at this capacity
I couldn't quite
see beyond...

totally missed
the depth of
his pain...

his desire to
pass it on

and me,
standing there,
– blind receiver.

just fine

That's ok.
I can miss you
quietly.

It won't last
for always;

& I'll be just fine.

the way I miss you

The way I miss you
isn't a normal way
of missing.

It's more of a
who left who?
did I leave
or did you?

& who
pushed who
... away?

too many
questions

& not enough
closure

q and a

In my mind,
I keep answering
all of the questions
that you never
even asked.

let go

& you have to
let go
because
he can't know
that you
need him.

a refusal

I still don't
understand your
disappearance,
but I refuse
to waste time
wondering.

I won't
give breath
to the question

of whether
you were real.

empty space

& it seems so dangerous...
so horribly risky
letting someone fill the space…

because, if they don't stay
(even if you know
they need to go)

the space
they leave behind
seems much more   empty
much more hollow…

& somehow
more permanent

than the space
before they came.

untitled

my thoughts
reach out
to find you,
and come back
empty-handed.

I wonder -

will I miss
missing you
once I've let you
fade away?

know this

Know this, and remember:
he's not the only one
who'll ever see you.

He's not the only one.

Please, don't
go on believing
he's the only one.

He's just
the only one
you can see
right now.

If he doesn't
make you feel loved
the way you deserve
to feel loved

If you spend
time and energy
puzzling over him;
trying to make him
okay enough...

Walk away.

validation

If I need you
to validate my worth...
then I must feel
worthless without you...

& that's just not ok.

mutual

I keep remembering...
yeah, I left too,
whenever I wonder
what happened to you.

no such thing

in real life.

Yeah, that's exactly it.
It's like we don't exist.

When I look back
I can hardly even
      see us.

Imagination's
figments.
no such thing
      as us.

lightened shades

I'll still be looking,
but with lightened
shades of hope;
and one day,
sort of random-like,
there you'll be.

reset

truth
be told,
you never
should've
been here.

note to self:
 restore
  defaults.

delete / block

the madness does
have a method;
seeking the source
within each source
    systematically.
glance, search, select –
delete, block, unsubscribe.

You have been
crowding my space.

damage control

I've been trying
to forget you
for so long...
I forgot
that's what
I was doing.

Every choice
I've made
(since you)
has always been
about you...

twenty years of
damage control

& you never intended
to break me...

circumstance

I wonder if I
ever cross your mind
the way that you cross mine.

    2 strangers ...
    the outcome of
    circumstance
    & time gone by,

        each, unable
           to forget
                the other.

it's funny

It's funny how I
need you with one breath
and forget you with the next.

– lifted –

sleeping superhumans

it's not fake it till you make it.
it's more like sink or swim;
...more like
  fight or flight.

it's survival.

daily hoping
you make it through

It's putting on airs
in the worst of ways,
It's coping and
coping
and coping so much,
til you forget
what it is
not to be
surviving

You smile
because it's better.
You move forward
because you know
you can't stand still,

and you're
horrified

to fall back.

It's like swatting at thoughts and fear.
It's gulping down what ifs
hoping that you won't choke…

You can't fake anything...
Fake isn't the word.

You just keep going.

You don't fake it till you make it.
You defy reality.

You become superhuman.
You become something
akin to
autopilot.

But the
programming
is so
deliberate.

Avoid destruction.
Avoid destruction.
Avoid destruction.

the mind repeats like a pulse

it's what keeps you going

Get up. Get up...
Move. You can do this.
Yes, you can. Get up.

Go.

The hell with "want to."
You have no options really.

It's forward or death,
it seems.

So you keep going.
You don't fake it till you make it.

You wake up everyday,
you do the impossible,
because you have to
and it's so horrifying.

Jesus, it's so horrifying.

We just want to rest.

Please hold us up
when we grow weary....
Forgive us for trying
to do it all alone.

We don't know
what else to do.

We've learned *cope* and *survive*
like the back of our hands,
Like our ABCs…

We've memorized
fear and *desperation*
like a lullaby
rocking us to sleep…

All day long...
always...
Sleeping Superhumans
running from reality
in slow motion.

Ready, Set, Go.
Go. Go. Go.

because you have to.

undeniable beauty

It doesn't
have to be pretty
to be true

In fact...

it seems:
the most
undeniable beauty

lives in the
ugliest truths

you are Phoenix

Do you have ANY idea
how MIRACULOUS you are?
...how IMPOSSIBLE life is
for you right now....?
yet you
keep.
on.
going.

Some days
feel like
the end of
everything.

Some days,
you may wonder
what you're doing wrong.

You may wonder if you'll
EVER get it right;

if you'll ever touch
your hopes and dreams.

I hope you realize
YOU'RE NOT
DOING
ANYTHING
WRONG…

You are rebuilding yourself
from ashes,

the result of
the fire
you refused
to feel....

though your
personal furnace
singed, burned,
and destroyed...

Yes...
my God, yes;
this is hard.

it's damn near
impossible.

but you are Phoenix.

Keep rising.
Keep building.

build to last

Take your time.
Yes, build.
but don't rush
the construction.

build
   strong
   real
   to last.

be.

be dope
be fly
be the sun
moon & stars;

not because I say so,
not because you can –
but because

you are.

go ahead and dance

you might as well
go ahead
and dance
in the car.

those people...
in those other cars...
they don't even know you.

maybe they'll laugh at you.
So what? What does it matter?
they don't. even. know you.

& anyway; maybe…
…maybe they'll catch
a bit of joy.

trust the process

Believe in your own wings.
though you might not see them yet,
or even feel them emerging...
trust your transition;
trust the process.

Challenge every doubt
and every thought that rises up
against your ultimate success.

Tell the voice inside your head
it is not your master, nor your blueprint –
unless the voice lines up
with your transition...

then, stand and wait, expectantly,
knowing, you can (and will)
become every bit of who you are
intended to become.

let it rest

If you're not sure,
wait.
Don't rush.
Let it rest
where it is.

You can always
come
back to it.

24 hours

& who
ever said
you had to
do it all
today?

& what
made you
believe
them?

soon enough

Keep moving forward.
intentional. deliberate.
Soon enough, you'll step
right into who you are.

masterpiece

upgrade.
level up.
progress.
maintain.
reflect.
anticipate.
move forward.
grow.
evolve.
become.

& only look back
to marvel at
the distance
which
you have traveled.

you, my dear,
are a masterpiece.

Like Cast Iron Butterflies

Since when...
did butterflies
come formed from
cast iron
and steel?

How did beautiful strength
cripple hope?

gentle, soft and mild,
fluttering to and fro,
pausing to build
bridges, fortresses, lives...
escaping harm with ease

but so fragile...
and so damn strong

No one seems aware
the struggle
in being so....
Strong.

none but other
steel beauties:
rock solid like water....
Yeah, that's it, exactly...
rock solid, like water
strong, and determined,
but delicate…

Handle with care.

We're like cast iron butterflies,
yet we fly with such grace.

If you look closely
you might discover....

more butterfly.... less rock.

Don't hold on too tightly.

If it doesn't make you happy... If it doesn't bring you peace...

If you look closely and can see you have the choice to do so: let it go.

Relax, Relate, Release.
Let. It. Go.

If it's yours, it's yours. It will always be yours. But maybe now's not the time. Maybe this isn't the way to get there.

Sometimes, we start down certain paths, full of so much excitement and dedication, we tend to forget the possibilities.... What if the path you are so dedicated to exists merely to lead you toward another path? What if you had to travel the distance you've traveled, just so you could see what you couldn't see from where you started the journey?

Don't hold on too tight. Always be cognizant of forks in the road...

Detours become opportunities. If you let them.

Let's Connect.

I am available for speaking engagements, poetry readings, conferences, and coaching.

I would love to hear your story, and walk along with you on your journey.

Please reach out via e-mail to
castironbutterfly77@gmail.com

Visit my blog: https://castironbutterfly.wordpress.com/

Or look me up on social media:
Instagram: @sylphina_angel_77 and @sylphina_writes
Facebook Page: @CastIronButterfly

Peace and Blessings to you.
- mykal k.w.

Made in the USA
Middletown, DE
09 August 2019